This Planner Belongs to

_____

2020
Christmas Organizing Planner

Created by

Krisann Blair
Christmas Coach & Christmas Organizing Founder

Cassandra Cooper
Editor & Author Assistant

Ashlyn Blair
Editor

2020 Christmas Organizing Planner

Copyright © Krisann Blair 2020
Jackson, TN 38301

ISBN 9798670404976

Independently Published

Dedication

God
First and foremost, I dedicate this and all my work to God. Without the gifts and guidance from God, I would be lost, and without His most precious gift, Jesus Christ, we would not have a Christmas to celebrate each year.

Ashley
My husband and my best friend, who encourages and supports me daily in so many ways.

Ashlyn
My newest editor and social media expert to help me take Christmas Organizing to new heights.

Aaron & Destiny
My son and daughter-in-law for helping with errands and little things that add up so I can continue to write.

My Mother
The memory of my mother and Christmas time is my foundation for what I do. She instilled in me the love for Christmas and showed me the true meaning of Christmas as a child and as an adult. She believed in my writing even when I did not.

Cassandra, Darla, Lori (in memory) & Susan
Special thanks to special people who were behind the scenes "elves" on this and other projects in various ways – editing, moderating, idea bouncing, being my friend and so much more than I can mention. Thank you for believing in me!

Special Thanks

The following people have joined Christmas Organizing
as founding members through Patreon.   Thank you for your support!

Santa & Book Sponsors

Susan G.   Mary Ann M.   Jonathon S.   Jacqulynn B.   Cassandra C.

Founding Patrons

Coffee   Donna B.   Ashlyn B.   Lorie K.   Barbara D.   Kim G.   Gena W.

Lori S.   Jenny W.   Carol B.   Joyce R.   Terry K.   Cynthia M.   Cindy R.

Contents

Meet Krisann, Christmas Coach

Author | Speaker | Christmas Organizing Founder

My Story

During the Christmas of 1998, I discovered that in all the busyness of the season, I had missed the Spirit of Christmas. Resolving never to let that happen again, I set out on a journey to make my Christmas a time of peace, joy, and family celebrations. In this process, I founded Christmas Organizing.com to be able to share with others my insights to a more JOYful Christmas season. You are invited to allow me to share ideas and encouragement for you to calm the Christmas chaos and take your Christmas from stressed to blessed.

Christmas has always been an important part of my life, and my mother always made it extra special, even from my very first Christmas. I am originally from Mannington, WV and I currently reside in Jackson, TN, with my husband, Ashley, and children Ashlyn and Aaron and my daughter-in-law Destiny.

Traveling is one of our favorite family activities, and we love Disney (especially cruising) and one of my favorite times at Disney is Christmas. I am also involved in our local FCE Extension Club (Family & Community Education), Christmas Cottage, 4-H, LANA (our neighborhood group), D.A.R., and our church. Besides Christmas, my favorite hobbies include crafting, cooking, family research, card games, and puzzles.

Throughout the years I have been asked to speak at churches, writer's conferences, Christmas stores, and have been featured on radio and television. I love to teach others about embracing the Christmas season and creating a plan for a less stressful holiday season. I have been honored to be featured in Entrepreneur Magazine as an Intel Road Warrior, USA Today newspaper, Women's World Magazine and other local publications.

How Christmas Organizing Began . . .

The Christmas of 1998 changed the way I approached Christmas because it was a disaster. If you look at our pictures from that year, you would never know it. The pictures in the album show happy kids opening gifts in the floor by the Christmas tree. But photographs do not tell the whole story. What you do not know is that early Christmas morning before the kids got up, I decorated only the bottom of the tree as that was all that would show up in the pictures. We had cereal for breakfast instead of our traditional breakfast casserole. Gifts were missing because I ran out of time to purchase some, and others were lost somewhere in the house. The greatest disappointment for me, though, was that for the first time we missed Christmas eve church services. All this plus other small things left me feeling like a failure that Christmas. The worst thing was that I knew how to plan for Christmas because my mother had taught me through all the years growing up. She loved Christmas, and she always made it joyful and special no matter what. That is when I decided I needed to put what my mother taught me into action.

Christmas Organizing was started in December of 1998 just days after Christmas as a way for people to "gather" online via a message board to support each other in getting and staying organized for Christmas through year-long planning. I shared Christmas tips and challenges each day with the group. What I started all those years ago as a way to keep me focused has turned into a love and passion for teaching and helping others have the Christmas season they desire!

To learn more, visit www.ChristmasOrganizing.com

The Christmas Organizing Planning System

Twenty plus years ago, Christmas Organizing started with the focus of creating a Christmas notebook to create a central location as a landing spot for Christmas planning and ideas. One important aspect of Christmas planning is creating lists and planning pages to organize all the different aspects of Christmas. Over the years, I have created over 100+ Christmas planning pages available to download and print to form the basis of the Christmas Organizing Notebook.

This year I was asked to create a dated, printed-bound planner by one of my dearest friends. I loved the idea, especially since I encourage everyone to remove specific pages from their notebook each year after Christmas and put them in an envelope with the year for later reference.

This request put me on a journey to create the planner you have. Due to a large number of planning pages and the need for multiple copies of some pages, the original idea turned into almost 300 pages – way too large for this project. As I pondered how to prioritize the sheets to a manageable size to be bound, I realized that there were two categories of planning pages. One category is the pages we fill out every year and the other was planning pages that rarely change. Two worlds become one!

With a clear direction, the Christmas Organizing Planner was developed and now we have multiple sections of Christmas Organizing . The planner is dated and filled with the planning pages that you typically change each year. The Christmas Organizing Planner can be slid into a

3-ring Christmas binder and can easily removed and carried with you in a purse or tote bag while on-the-go. Then, at the end of the Christmas season, you can tuck this planner away easily for future reference.

Now the question is, "what will be in the 3-ring binder"? The binder is not gone! It will play a slightly different role. With the introduction of the Christmas Organizing Planner in a printed, bound format, we have the opportunity to rework the Christmas Organizing system and blend the two aspects to help with Christmas planning even more!

The printed-bound planner has the primary Christmas planning pages for the current holiday season that will differ from year to year in most cases.

Visit www.ChristmasOrganizing.com for more information on downloading supplemental planning pages that do not change from year to year to print out on your printer and put in your 3-ring binder. These planning pages include Favorite Foods, Gift Ideas, Theme Ideas, Decorating Plan, family favorite interview pages, and more! Many of the supplemental forms are free to download, or you can become a Candy Cane Club member and have access to all the planning pages, current and new, throughout the year included with your $1 monthly membership for 2020 (limited time price).

The Christmas Organizing website has tips, ideas, and resources to help you populate your 3-ring binder with recipes, craft ideas, decorating samples, and more!

Lastly, don't forget to purchase your 2021 Christmas Organizing planner.

Christmas Reflections

Why do you need to reflect about Christmas? Simple, when you write things down, it helps to put them in focus – the good and the bad.

Christmas is a joyous season and should not be dreaded but CELEBRATED. Each family has their ways of celebrating Christmas. Symbols, activities, and traditions mean different things to different people during the season. Christmas is not about doing what the "world" tells us to do. It is about celebrating Christ's birth in a way your family grasps the meaning the most.

Take time to think about the Christmas season! Many times, we do not think about Christmas; we just "do it," which can lead to disappointments and many "I wish I had done this or done that" after the season. The first step is to reflect on what did not go as planned so you can find solutions to the issue. The second thing to reflect on is to write out a list of things that went as planned and that you want to repeat for the upcoming Christmas season.

Remember to answer the questions truthfully. There is no right or wrong answer.

Reflecting on Christmas Past

Answer the following questions:

Do you enjoy the Christmas season? Why or Why not? List out the main items that caused you stress.	
Does your Christmas seem out of control with things just happening without rhyme or reason, and do you spend more time looking for your lists, recipes, gifts, etc. than you spend with family during Christmas?	
Do you overspend during Christmas? If so, in what areas?	
Do you ask your family to help with preparations for the Christmas season?	
Do you buy gifts throughout the year, only to lose them when it comes time to wrap the gifts?	
Did you send Christmas cards this past year? Did it go as planned? If you did not send cards, did you want to?	
Do you purchase gifts with a purpose, with the recipient in mind? If not, do you want to?	
Would you like to entertain more (or even at all) during the holiday season?	
Are there activities you did not do this past year that you wanted to do? Are there activities that did not go as planned?	
Did you overbook yourself this past Christmas?	
What is one thing you would change about this past Christmas?	
What is one thing you would NOT change about this Christmas?	

Last Christmas: What Went Wrong?

Make a list of things that did not go as planned and briefly describe what happened and what could be done this year to create success.

What did not go as planned?	What happened? What can you do differently this year?

Last Christmas: What Worked?

Make a list of things that went as planned and briefly describe what happened and any adjustments you need to make for this year.

What went as planned?	Any adjustments for this year?

Foundations of Christmas Planning
Christmas Calendar

Preparing a Christmas Calendar may seem like a basic thing to do, but it is a crucial step in your Christmas planning. Even if Christmas is still months away, you need to start thinking about your holiday calendar now because it is an essential way of reducing holiday stress. Your calendar will serve as your road map for the upcoming season.

There are many online and software programs available to print out customized calendars, and I highly suggest using one. Using a computer-based calendar will allow you to input reoccurring things like your sister's birthday (and some programs can even tell you how old she will be that year!) as well as when lay-a-way payments are due and when the kids get out for the holiday break. Calendars with personalized dates on them also make great gifts that everyone loves! Even though I love the computer calendars that I can print out, whatever type of calendar you have will work as long as there is space to add your events.

You can also use the Christmas Planning calendar page included and fill it in for September through December. Using these calendar sheets is a great way to start recording things you know will come up before placing them into your daily calendar.

Christmas Calendar Dates

Use this form for family member events scheduled in December so you can add it to your calendar. Ask your family to alert you to dates of events or activities as soon as they know them. If you have an event you know will happen, but do not know the date yet, go ahead and list it on this form.

Date of Event & Name of Submitter	Event Information Time, Place, Gift Needed, etc.

September 2020

Sunday	Monday	Tuesday	Wednesday	Thursday	Friday	Saturday
		1	2	3	4	5
6	7	8	9	10	11	12
13	14	15	16	17	18	19
20	21	22	23	24	25	26
27	28	29	30			

October 2020

Sunday	Monday	Tuesday	Wednesday	Thursday	Friday	Saturday
				1	2	3
4	5	6	7	8	9	10
11	12	13	14	15	16	17
18	19	20	21	22	23	24
25	26	27	28	29	30	31

November 2020

Sunday	Monday	Tuesday	Wednesday	Thursday	Friday	Saturday
1	2	3	4	5	6	7
8	9	10	11	12	13	14
15	16	17	18	19	20	21
22	23	24	25	26	27	28
29	30					

December 2020

Sunday	Monday	Tuesday	Wednesday	Thursday	Friday	Saturday
		1	2	3	4	5
6	7	8	9	10	11	12
13	14	15	16	17	18	19
20	21	22	23	24	25	26
27	28	29	30	31		

Foundations of Christmas Planning
Christmas Saving & Spending

Christmas is a time when many people throw caution to the wind and buy what they think will make everyone else happy—often charging the purchases, to deal with the outcome in January. This is not a good strategy because it only causes more stress. With planning, you can map out your expected expenses and put back money throughout the year to help with expenses in December.

Use the planning forms in this section to help you map out your Christmas saving and spending for the year.

Christmas Expenses

Use this page to write down and budget out different items you spend money on at Christmas.

	Christmas Category	Budget Amount
1	Christmas Offering at Church	
2	Charity Donations	
3	Decorations	
4	Gifts for Family	
5	Gifts for Friends	
6	Entertaining	
7	Baking	
8	Christmas Cards	
9	Dinners Out in December	
10	Postage (for shipping packages and mailing cards)	
11	Christmas Pictures	
12	Cleaning Services	
13	Travel (gas, hotel, food, etc.)	
14		
15		
16		

Christmas Expenses

Use this page to write down and budget out different items you spend money on at Christmas.

	Christmas Category	Budget Amount
1		
2		
3		
4		
5		
6		
7		
8		
9		
10		
11		
12		
13		
14		
15		
16		

Christmas Spending Ledger

Create one sheet for each category of your Christmas expenses. Record purchases and keep a running total of how much you have spent.

Category: _____ Amount Budgeted: _____

Item Purchased	Amount Spent	Balance

Christmas Spending Ledger

Create one sheet for each category of your Christmas expenses. Record purchases and keep a running total of how much you have spent.

Category: Amount Budgeted:

Item Purchased	Amount Spent	Balance

Christmas Spending Ledger

Category: **Amount Budgeted:**

Item Purchased	Amount Spent	Balance

Category: **Amount Budgeted:**

Item Purchased	Amount Spent	Balance

Category: **Amount Budgeted:**

Item Purchased	Amount Spent	Balance

Christmas Spending Ledger

Category: **Amount Budgeted:**

Item Purchased	Amount Spent	Balance

Category: **Amount Budgeted:**

Item Purchased	Amount Spent	Balance

Category: **Amount Budgeted:**

Item Purchased	Amount Spent	Balance

Christmas Spending Ledger

Category: **Amount Budgeted:**

Item Purchased	Amount Spent	Balance

Category: **Amount Budgeted:**

Item Purchased	Amount Spent	Balance

Category: **Amount Budgeted:**

Item Purchased	Amount Spent	Balance

Christmas Spending Ledger

Category: **Amount Budgeted:**

Item Purchased	Amount Spent	Balance

Category: **Amount Budgeted:**

Item Purchased	Amount Spent	Balance

Category: **Amount Budgeted:**

Item Purchased	Amount Spent	Balance

Charity Ideas

Make a list of charities that you want to consider donating to this Christmas season. Once you decide on a charity, complete a charity information sheet.

Charity Name	Volunteer	Money Donation	Supplies/Items Donation	Can Children Participate?

Charity Information Sheet

Name of Charity

What type of programs do they have?	
Is the charity a 501C3?	
Mailing Address	
Phone Number	
Do they send cards for donations in Memory/Honor?	
Do they have a local chapter or office?	
How are the donated funds used?	
Do they need supplies, money, or time donated?	
Do they have any special programs at Christmas?	
Ages allowed to volunteer?	
What are the times that volunteers are needed?	

Charity Information Sheet

Name of Charity

What type of programs do they have?	
Is the charity a 501C3?	
Mailing Address	
Phone Number	
Do they send cards for donations in Memory/Honor?	
Do they have a local chapter or office?	
How are the donated funds used?	
Do they need supplies, money, or time donated?	
Do they have any special programs at Christmas?	
Ages allowed to volunteer?	
What are the times that volunteers are needed?	

Gift Lists

Gifts @ Christmas
Christmas Gift Lists

Gift-giving can be a frustrating process if you do not keep a complete list of the people you would like to give gifts to during the Christmas season, including yourself! This section contains planning pages to create gift lists for everyone, including ideas and selected gifts. The first list you need to make is for yourself of things YOU would like to get for Christmas. By keeping a personal list, when others ask you what you would like for Christmas, you can give them ideas, just like when you ask them for ideas!

On your Master Gift List planning page, write down EVERYONE you want to give a gift to this year if money and time were not an issue.   While you are making your list, classify each person on your list. The classification system is: A=Must give a gift, B=Want to give a gift, C= Will give a gift if possible.

Take your master list and separate it into Gifting Groups based on recipients, using a separate sheet for each group. Gifting Groups are sheets which contain recipients who are related to each other. Examples would include co-workers, Sunday school members, neighbors, close friends, cousins, etc. Using your Master Gift List, begin filling in your sheets based on each person's assigned group.   As you transfer names, write down any gift ideas you may have for that person.

My Christmas List

Ideas to give others when they ask ME what I want!

Gift Idea	Store/Website	Price Range

Master Gift List

Name	Group	Classification

Master Gift List

Name	Group	Classification

Gift List – Group:

Name	Gift Ideas	Gift Selected	Purchased	Wrapped	Mailed	Given	Classification

Gift List – Group:

Name	Gift Ideas	Gift Selected	Purchased	Wrapped	Mailed	Given	Classification

Gift List – Group:

Name	Gift Ideas	Gift Selected	Purchased	Wrapped	Mailed	Given	Classification

Gift List – Group:

Name	Gift Ideas	Gift Selected	Purchased	Wrapped	Mailed	Given	Classification

Gift List – Group:

Name	Gift Ideas	Gift Selected	Purchased	Wrapped	Mailed	Given	Classification

Gift List – Group:

Name	Gift Ideas	Gift Selected	Purchased	Wrapped	Mailed	Given	Classification

Stocking Gifts

Recipient:

Gift Ideas	Gift Selected	Purchased	Wrapped	Mailed	Given	

Stocking Gifts

Recipient:

Gift Ideas	Gift Selected	Purchased	Wrapped	Mailed	Given	

www.ChristmasOrganizing.com

Stocking Gifts

Recipient:

Gift Ideas	Gift Selected	Purchased	Wrapped	Mailed	Given	

Stocking Gifts

Recipient:

Gift Ideas	Gift Selected	Purchased	Wrapped	Mailed	Given	

More Than One Gift

Gifts For:

Gift Ideas	Gift Selected	Purchased	Wrapped	Mailed	Given	

More Than One Gift

Gifts For:

Gift Ideas	Gift Selected	Purchased	Wrapped	Mailed	Given	

More Than One Gift

Gifts For:

Gift Ideas	Gift Selected	Purchased	Wrapped	Mailed	Given	

www.ChristmasOrganizing.com

More Than One Gift

Gifts For:

Gift Ideas	Gift Selected	Purchased	Wrapped	Mailed	Given	

Christmas Gift Shopping

Christmas shopping. What comes to mind for you when you hear those two words together? For most people, it is either a sinking feeling in their stomach or excitement, but also knowing that if you plan to give gifts, you must complete this task. Giving gifts to people, in my opinion, is truly a labor of love because most of us put thought into the gifts we buy and do not just head out to the store with no idea of what someone would like.

Using your Gifting Groups form, make a Christmas Gift Shopping List of gifts you need to purchase once you have decided on a gift for each person. It can be helpful to make multiple copies and write the specific store/event/website on the top and then list all the gifts you need from that location.

If you will be shopping online or using lay-a-way, use the Internet Purchase Tracking and Lay-a-Way Tracker planning pages to track your internet and lay-a-way purchases. These pages will come in handy close to Christmas.

Christmas Gift Shopping List

Use this form to make a shopping list of gifts you need to buy and what store/event/website the item can be found.

Gift to Purchase	Store/Event/Website	Gift for:

Christmas Gift Shopping List

Use this form to make a shopping list of gifts you need to buy and what store/event/website the item can be found.

Gift to Purchase	Store/Event/Website	Gift for:

Internet Purchase Tracking

Website:	Items Ordered:
Date Ordered	
Gift for	
Expected Delivery Date	
Shipping Method	
Shipping Carrier	
Confirmation Number	
Shipment Tracking Number	
Phone Number	

Website:	Items Ordered:
Date Ordered	
Gift for	
Expected Delivery Date	
Shipping Method	
Shipping Carrier	
Confirmation Number	
Shipment Tracking Number	
Phone Number	

Internet Purchase Tracking

Website:	Items Ordered:
Date Ordered	
Gift for	
Expected Delivery Date	
Shipping Method	
Shipping Carrier	
Confirmation Number	
Shipment Tracking Number	
Phone Number	

Website:	Items Ordered:
Date Ordered	
Gift for	
Expected Delivery Date	
Shipping Method	
Shipping Carrier	
Confirmation Number	
Shipment Tracking Number	
Phone Number	

Internet Purchase Tracking

Website:	Items Ordered:
Date Ordered	
Gift for	
Expected Delivery Date	
Shipping Method	
Shipping Carrier	
Confirmation Number	
Shipment Tracking Number	
Phone Number	

Website:	Items Ordered:
Date Ordered	
Gift for	
Expected Delivery Date	
Shipping Method	
Shipping Carrier	
Confirmation Number	
Shipment Tracking Number	
Phone Number	

Internet Purchase Tracking

Website:	Items Ordered:
Date Ordered	
Gift for	
Expected Delivery Date	
Shipping Method	
Shipping Carrier	
Confirmation Number	
Shipment Tracking Number	
Phone Number	

Website:	Items Ordered:
Date Ordered	
Gift for	
Expected Delivery Date	
Shipping Method	
Shipping Carrier	
Confirmation Number	
Shipment Tracking Number	
Phone Number	

Lay-A-Way Tracker

Store Name	
Date Placed	
Final Payment Date	

Items in Lay-A-Way

Gifts @ Christmas
Christmas Gift Storage

Have you ever looked under the bed, in the closets, in your car, anywhere you can think of to find that gift you know you purchased way back in March because it was the perfect Christmas gift for your best friend? This is a genuine problem for many people who buy gifts throughout the year if there is not a single collection point to place the gifts when they are purchased. Once you have a location selected, you need to take inventory of all the gifts you have, both unassigned and assigned.

Using the Purchased Gift Inventory form, record gifts you have bought but are not assigned and are waiting for you to give as a gift - you know those gifts you cannot pass up because the price is excellent and you will find someone to give it to on your list!

When you assign a gift from your inventory form, put the information on the Assigned Gift Inventory form. This will help you know what is for who when it comes time to start wrapping. Don't forget to cross the item off your inventory form, so you know it is no longer up for grabs. If you bring a gift home that you already know who you are giving it to, write it directly onto this form and then place it into your gifting collection area. Consider having a separate box for assigned items to help keep items divided.

Purchased Gift Inventory

Gift items purchased but not assigned. Cross items off this list as you assign them.

Assigned Gift Inventory

Items you have purchased for a specific recipient

Item	Recipient	Occasion	Wrapping: Box? Bag? Paper?

Assigned Gift Inventory

Items you have purchased for a specific recipient

Item	Recipient	Occasion	Wrapping: Box? Bag? Paper?

Gifts @ Christmas
Gift Wrapping & Mailing

Most people either love to wrap gifts or think of it as a chore. Some people decorate with elaborate bows, ribbons, and decorations while others put things in Christmas bags and call it a day! No matter how you wrap, you still need to do a few things to get yourself organized so you are not handing over your gifts in a plastic grocery bag!

Your first task is to go around and gather all your wrapping supplies in one location. Use the Gift Wrapping Supplies form to note how many of each type of supply you have on hand.

If you purchase and use gift bags, use the Gift Bag Supplies form to list out gift bags by material and size that you have on hand. This will help you to organize what you have and what you need. Under specialty bags, list out things such as cellophane bags, extra-large gift bags, treat bags, etc. that you use during the holiday season.

Use the Packages to Mail form to make a list of packages you need to mail. It is essential to know how many gifts you need to send and try to consolidate shipping to as few locations as possible. For example, if everyone goes to a particular house during the season, mail all the gifts there to be picked up when they visit. This approach will help with mailing costs for Christmas.

Gift Wrapping Supplies

Supplies	# on hand	# Needed
Wrapping Paper		
Tape		
Scissors		
Name Tags		
Bags		
Boxes		
Bows		

Other Items

Christmas Gift Bag Supplies

Gift Bag Size	# on hand	# Needed

Specialty Bags

Specialty Bags		

Wrapping Supplies Shopping List

Item	Quantity Needed	Purchased	Item	Quantity Needed	Purchased

Wrapping Supplies Shopping List

Item	Quantity Needed	Purchased	Item	Quantity Needed	Purchased

Packages to Mail

Make a list of packages you will need to mail. Indicate the date it needs to arrive and how you will be sending each package. Consult with the shipper to see how many days in advance you need to mail the package and put the information on your Christmas Organizing Calendar.

Family/Person Receiving Package	Date Package Needs to Arrive	Post Office	UPS	Fed Ex	Other

Gifts @ Christmas

Christmas Cards

For many people, sending Christmas cards is their way of sending a small gift to their friends and family. With a little planning, you can send the one card to everyone that becomes his or her favorite and is kept for years to come.

How many cards do you want to send? Hundreds of people or just your immediate family or somewhere in between? Knowing this is important because it can affect your time and money during the Christmas season. Now is the time to make out your Christmas Card List. Don't forget, just like your gift list, classify your card list and begin addressing and sending those with your "A" or number 1 category first. Once your list is complete, locate addresses and create Christmas Contact Cards or add them to your existing address book.

Do you want to include a Christmas letter? Use the Christmas Newsletter Monthly Information form to write down the top three things that happen each month of the year to work into your note. This is a great way also to get your family involved because you can ask them what they want others to know about this past year and add the information to the form.

Christmas Card List

Name (include all household names)	In address book?	Classification

Christmas Card List

Name (include all household names)	In address book?	Classification

Christmas Card Supplies

Supplies	# on hand	# Needed
Cards		
Stamps		
Pen		
Return Address Labels		
Christmas Letter Paper		
Extra Envelopes		
Stickers		

Other Items

Christmas Newsletter Monthly Information

Month: _____

Three things that happened this month:

1 _____

2 _____

3 _____

Month: _____

Three things that happened this month:

1 _____

2 _____

3 _____

Month: _____

Three things that happened this month:

1 _____

2 _____

3 _____

Christmas Newsletter Monthly Information

Month: _____

Three things that happened this month:

1 _____

2 _____

3 _____

Month: _____

Three things that happened this month:

1 _____

2 _____

3 _____

Month: _____

Three things that happened this month:

1 _____

2 _____

3 _____

Christmas Newsletter Monthly Information

Month: _____

Three things that happened this month:

1 _____

2 _____

3 _____

Month: _____

Three things that happened this month:

1 _____

2 _____

3 _____

Month: _____

Three things that happened this month:

1 _____

2 _____

3 _____

Christmas Newsletter Monthly Information

Month: _____

Three things that happened this month:

  1 _____

  2 _____

  3 _____

Month: _____

Three things that happened this month:

  1 _____

  2 _____

  3 _____

Month: _____

Three things that happened this month:

  1 _____

  2 _____

  3 _____

Christmas Crafting

No matter if you want to start a new craft you found on Pinterest this year, or finish craft projects you started last year, you need to fill out a Craft Project form. The purpose of this form is to help you understand the full scope of each craft project you want to make.

Many times we think of crafts as being quick and easy and less expensive, but sometimes there is nothing further from the truth! For each project you want to make as a gift, make ONE first and record how long it took you to complete and what the total cost to make one would be. By knowing how much time you will need to create one item, you can evaluate if you have enough time left to complete 20 or only 5, allowing you to assign the craft as a gift accordingly.

If your idea came from a website, print out the information or tear out the pages from your magazine and place it in your Christmas notebook in a sheet protector. If your idea comes from a craft book, in the directions section, write the name of the book, the name of the project, and the page number where it can be found, allowing you to quickly find the directions when you are ready to begin working.

Don't forget to write down the date you need to have the project completed and add it to your Christmas calendar.

Crafts to Make for Christmas

Craft Idea	Details	New Craft	Craft Already Started

Craft Project

Complete this form for each Christmas craft project you will be doing this year.

Craft	
How many to make for gifts	
Amount of time to make each one	
Sample location (book, web site)	

Supplies Needed

Directions or Comments

Date to be completed by:	
Notes	

Craft Project

Complete this form for each Christmas craft project you will be doing this year.

Craft	
How many to make for gifts	
Amount of time to make each one	
Sample location (book, web site)	

Supplies Needed

Directions or Comments

Date to be completed by:	
Notes	

Craft Project

Complete this form for each Christmas craft project you will be doing this year.

Craft	
How many to make for gifts	
Amount of time to make each one	
Sample location (book, web site)	

Supplies Needed

Directions or Comments

Date to be completed by:	
Notes	

Craft Project

Complete this form for each Christmas craft project you will be doing this year.

Craft	
How many to make for gifts	
Amount of time to make each one	
Sample location (book, web site)	

Supplies Needed

Directions or Comments

Date to be completed by:	
Notes	

Craft Project

Complete this form for each Christmas craft project you will be doing this year.

Craft	
How many to make for gifts	
Amount of time to make each one	
Sample location (book, web site)	

Supplies Needed

Directions or Comments

Date to be completed by:	
Notes	

Christmas Crafting Shopping List

Use this form to make a shopping list of craft items you need to buy and what store/website the item is located.

Craft Supply to Purchase	Store/Website	Craft

Christmas Kitchen
Baking & Special Meals

During Christmas, we often find ourselves in the kitchen more than other times of the year. From baking goodies to cooking special meals for family and friends, the time you spend in your kitchen should be joyful and not stressful. For this reason, you must do some planning.

Use the form Must-Have Christmas Foods to make a list of the foods you and your family "must" have during the Christmas season. The next form to fill out is the Christmas Food Plan for This Year to make a list of items you want to make and serve at home for the upcoming Christmas season. Use the form to plan the items and what activity or event they will be needed for this Christmas.

Use the form Make-Ahead Christmas Foods to make a list of foods that you want to have at Christmas that you can make ahead and will keep for an extended amount of time, or that you can freeze. By making this list, it will help keep you from making everything at the last minute.

Use the Christmas Food Supply List to make a list of the supplies you need for your baking and cooking for Christmas.

With a little planning, your Christmas foods can be memorable and not stressful!

Must-Have Christmas Foods

Make a list of the foods you and your family consider a "must" for Christmas. Indicate when you have the food listed. For example, homemade fudge at your Christmas Eve dinner or oranges in a bowl in the living room all season long.

Food	Occasion item is served/put out

Christmas Food Plan for This Year

Make a list of the foods you plan on serving this year during the Christmas season, along with the event or occasion you plan to serve the item.

Christmas Food	Event or Occasion

Christmas Food Plan for This Year

Make a list of the foods you plan on serving this year during the Christmas season, along with the event or occasion you plan to serve the item.

Christmas Food	Event or Occasion

Make-Ahead Christmas Foods

List out the foods you make for Christmas that can be made ahead of time. Examples: hot chocolate mix, canned items (such as jams), or frozen items (pumpkin bread).

Food Idea	How far in advance can this be made?

Christmas Food Supply List

Make a list of the supplies you need for your baking and cooking for Christmas. Include items that you need to purchase or have tucked away, so you are prepared when you are ready to cook or bake.

Food Item	Supplies Needed (indicate if you need to buy or only locate the item)

Christmas Kitchen
Food Gifts

During the Christmas season, many people give food gifts to those outside their immediate family. People love the idea of food gifts, and one reason is that we live in a world full of "stuff" and food as gifts do not leave "stuff" around after the holidays. Do you give food gifts at Christmas?

No matter if you plan on giving home-baked goodies or store-bought food items, let's do some planning!

One tip is to take a few minutes and call or send out a message via text, email, or Facebook to your friends and ask them if they have any food issues that might affect you giving food gifts. Use the form Christmas Food Gift List to create a list of the items you want to give as gifts this year. This list should include store-bought and homemade items.

Use the form Christmas Food Gifts to record all the information you need about EACH item you plan to make and give. Use a separate sheet for each item you are gifting. If you can make any of your food gifts in advance, use the form Make-Ahead Christmas Gift Foods to make a list of items that will keep for an extended amount of time, or that you can freeze.

Christmas Food Gift List

Make a list of the foods you plan to give as gifts this year.

Food Gift	Homemade or Store Bought?

Christmas Food Gifts

Food Item	
How many to make for gifts	
Amount of time to make each batch	
Yields	

Ingredients and Supplies (packaging) Needed

Recipe or Recipe Location and Comments

Date to be completed by	

Christmas Food Gifts

Food Item	
How many to make for gifts	
Amount of time to make each batch	
Yields	

Ingredients and Supplies (packaging) Needed

Recipe or Recipe Location and Comments

Date to be completed by	

Christmas Food Gifts

Food Item	
How many to make for gifts	
Amount of time to make each batch	
Yields	

Ingredients and Supplies (packaging) Needed

Recipe or Recipe Location and Comments

Date to be completed by	

Christmas Food Gifts

Food Item	
How many to make for gifts	
Amount of time to make each batch	
Yields	

Ingredients and Supplies (packaging) Needed

Recipe or Recipe Location and Comments

Date to be completed by	

Christmas Food Gifts

Food Item	
How many to make for gifts	
Amount of time to make each batch	
Yields	

Ingredients and Supplies (packaging) Needed

Recipe or Recipe Location and Comments

Date to be completed by	

Make-Ahead Christmas Food Gifts

List out the foods you make for Christmas food gifts that can be made ahead of time. Examples: hot chocolate mix, canned items (such as jams), or frozen items (pumpkin bread).

Food Idea	How far in advance can this be made?

Christmas Kitchen

December Dinners

December is a time filled with many activities and events. Our time runs short when it comes to cooking dinner every day. If you want to save money during December, plan your December dinners and do not get caught up in the "let's just eat out, I'm too tired" trap.

To help you make dinner decisions, use the form 30 Meals We Like to list out all the meals your family eats on "regular" nights. After you have filled out the list, get out your calendar and fill in meals for ALL of December. If December is still months away, fill in all the days you can and when activities or events come up, edit or remove the dinner from that night. If December is here (or very close) and you already have activities and events planned on your calendar, just fill in the days you need to plan for dinner.

Use the form Make-Ahead Dinners to make a list of the dinners from your 30 Meals that can be made ahead and will keep for an extended amount of time, or that you can freeze. By making this list, it will help keep you from making everything at the last minute, and your freezer will have a supply of dinners when you do not want to cook! Remember – it doesn't have to be the whole meal made ahead and frozen, it can be parts, and also think about doubling recipes in September, October, and November to put some aside for December.

30 Meals We Like (1-15)

Write down meals that your family likes to eat on a regular night.

	Meal	Slow Cooker or Freezer Friendly?
1		
2		
3		
4		
5		
6		
7		
8		
9		
10		
11		
12		
13		
14		
15		

30 Meals We Like (16-30)

	Meal	Slow Cooker or Freezer Friendly?
16		
17		
18		
19		
20		
21		
22		
23		
24		
25		
26		
27		
28		
29		
30		

Make-Ahead December Dinners

List out the foods you make for dinner that you can make ahead of time.

Food	How far in advance can this be made?

Christmas Kitchen
Grocery Shopping

Earlier you prepared lists of items for baking, family dinners, December dinners, and food gifts. Now is the time to look at those lists and start making your grocery shopping lists.

Use the Grocery Shopping List planing pages for your grocery shopping lists to keep track of items you may need. The pages in this section are for general grocery shopping and can also help you start shopping for non-perishable foods now, adding a few items to each grocery trip, so your food budget is not blown in December.

Go through each of your lists and find the corresponding recipes that you need for each item. Please make a copy of the recipe and place it in your notebook. Having a copy of the recipe will help you to keep track of the recipes you will be using during the upcoming Christmas season. Place the copies in a sheet protector so you can easily have it year after year in your notebook.

Break your lists out into perishable and non-perishable items so you can start buying some items NOW at the store, especially if you find them on sale.

Master Grocery Shopping List: Baking

List grocery items you need for baking during holiday home activities, not for gifts.

Non-Perishable Items	Purchased	Staple	Perishable Items	Purchased	Staple

Master Grocery Shopping List: Baking

List grocery items you need for baking during holiday home activities, not for gifts.

Non-Perishable Items	Purchased	Staple	Perishable Items	Purchased	Staple

Master Grocery Shopping List: Special Family Meals

List grocery items you need for special family meals. Examples: Advent Sunday Dinners, Christmas Eve Brunch, etc.

Non-Perishable Items	Purchased	Staple	Perishable Items	Purchased	Staple

Master Grocery Shopping List: Special Family Meals

List grocery items you need for special family meals. Examples: Advent Sunday Dinners, Christmas Eve Brunch, etc.

Non-Perishable Items	Purchased	Staple	Perishable Items	Purchased	Staple

Master Grocery Shopping List: December Dinners

List grocery items you need for your December dinners.

Non-Perishable Items	Purchased	Staple	Perishable Items	Purchased	Staple

Master Grocery Shopping List: December Dinners

List grocery items you need for your December dinners.

Non-Perishable Items	Purchased	Staple	Perishable Items	Purchased	Staple

Master Grocery Shopping List: December Dinners

List grocery items you need for your December dinners.

Non-Perishable Items	Purchased	Staple	Perishable Items	Purchased	Staple

Master Grocery Shopping List: Food Gifts

List grocery items you need for food related gifts you are giving for Christmas gifts.

Non-Perishable Items	Purchased	Staple	Perishable Items	Purchased	Staple

Master Grocery Shopping List: Food Gifts

List grocery items you need for food related gifts you are giving for Christmas gifts.

Non-Perishable Items	Purchased	Staple	Perishable Items	Purchased	Staple

Christmas Activities

Activities play an important role in celebrating the Christmas season because they allow us to actively participate in activities that bring out the true meaning of Christmas for us. For our planning purposes, activities are defined as things you do at your home with your immediate family and/or fewer than 5-10 people. Use the Entertaining section to plan out larger activities at your home. Events (which are covered later in this section) are things you do or attend away from home such as your holiday office party, Christmas Eve at your parents house, Christmas eve service at church, etc.

Decide what activities are a must-do this Christmas for you and your family. Do you host Christmas eve dinner at your house? Do you have a Christmas open house? Do you have a decorating party? Do you have a Christmas movie night with your kids? Make a list of all the activities you plan to do at home this year, and then for each one, fill out an activity planning sheet, including all the little details for each activity. If the activity includes more than 10 people, use the entertaining planning pages in the next section.

Christmas Activity List @ Home

List all the activities you are hosting at your home.

Activity	Date/Time of Event

Activity Planning Sheet - Home

Use this form to plan out activities you will be doing during the Christmas season at home.

Name of Activity	
Date of Activity	
Time of Activity	
Area of House for Activity	

Activity Details

Type of Activity (baking, crafting, game night)	
Budget for Activity	
Needed Activity Supplies	
Items for to bring (ornament exchange, dessert, gift, etc.)	
RSVP Deadline	

Additional Information About the Activity

People to invite:	Food to serve:

Activity Planning Sheet - Home

Use this form to plan out activities you will be doing during the Christmas season at home.

Name of Activity	
Date of Activity	
Time of Activity	
Area of House for Activity	

Activity Details

Type of Activity (baking, crafting, game night)	
Budget for Activity	
Needed Activity Supplies	
Items for to bring (ornament exchange, dessert, gift, etc.)	
RSVP Deadline	

Additional Information About the Activity

People to invite:	Food to serve:

Activity Planning Sheet - Home

Use this form to plan out activities you will be doing during the Christmas season at home.

Name of Activity	
Date of Activity	
Time of Activity	
Area of House for Activity	

Activity Details

Type of Activity (baking, crafting, game night)	
Budget for Activity	
Needed Activity Supplies	
Items for to bring (ornament exchange, dessert, gift, etc.)	
RSVP Deadline	

Additional Information About the Activity

People to invite:	Food to serve:

Activity Planning Sheet - Home

Use this form to plan out activities you will be doing during the Christmas season at home.

Name of Activity	
Date of Activity	
Time of Activity	
Area of House for Activity	

Activity Details

Type of Activity (baking, crafting, game night)	
Budget for Activity	
Needed Activity Supplies	
Items for to bring (ornament exchange, dessert, gift, etc.)	
RSVP Deadline	

Additional Information About the Activity

People to invite:	Food to serve:

Entertaining

Entertaining during Christmas can take on many forms. Invitations to parties, parties you host, family holiday get-togethers, etc. We might not consider many things we do entertaining but, for our planning purposes, any event you are hosting at your home with more than 5-10 people, we will classify as "entertaining."

Use the form Party Gathering List to make a list of any entertaining activities you will host at your home. These are not limited to formal parties only - include informal get-togethers (with more than 5-10 people) with close friends and family. The more we have written down, the less we will forget.

Use the Party Planning form to write down all the details for each activity you will be having at your home. Once you have all the details written out, decide on your guest list and use the Party Guest List form to create your guest list and track RSVP's. After you have your guest list it is time to use the Christmas Party Food form to do a menu plan for the activity. The last list to make out is a needed items list. Utilize the form Party/Entertaining "Need Items" to create a list of items you either need to locate, purchase, or borrow for the party and things that you can ask others to bring if they ask if there is anything they can bring.

Party/Gathering List

List any party or gathering you are hosting at your home.

Party or Gathering	Date/Time of Event

Party Details

Party Theme	
Date of Party	
Time of Party	
Location of Party	

Party Details

Number of People	
Who is the Party for?	
Party Favors?	
Items for attendees to bring (ornament exchange, etc.)	
RSVP Deadline	

Additional Information About the Party

Date to Send Invitations	

Party Guest List

Name	Phone/Email	Invitation Sent	RSVP - Yes	RSVP - No	Dietary Restrictions	Total Attending

Christmas Party Food

Event:

Type of Food	Food Item	Serving Dish Needed for Food Item	Will Make	Will Purchase	Ordered	Picked-Up

Party/Entertaining "Need Items"

Make a list of items you need to find or acquire or items that you may need help with at a party/gathering you are hosting. This list will allow you to know what you might need if someone asks, "can I bring anything?" Put this form with your party planning sheets for each party.

Item Needed	Person Bringing

Party Details

Party Theme	
Date of Party	
Time of Party	
Location of Party	

Party Details

Number of People	
Who is the Party for?	
Party Favors?	
Items for attendees to bring (ornament exchange, etc.)	
RSVP Deadline	

Additional Information About the Party

Date to Send Invitations	

Party Guest List

Name	Phone/Email	Invitation Sent	RSVP - Yes	RSVP - No	Dietary Restrictions	Total Attending

Christmas Party Food

Event:

Type of Food	Food Item	Serving Dish Needed for Food Item	Will Make	Will Purchase	Ordered	Picked-Up

Party/Entertaining "Need Items"

Make a list of items you need to find or acquire or items that you may need help with at a party/gathering you are hosting. This list will allow you to know what you might need if someone asks, "can I bring anything?" Put this form with your party planning sheets for each party.

Item Needed	Person Bringing

Party Details

Party Theme	
Date of Party	
Time of Party	
Location of Party	

Party Details

Number of People	
Who is the Party for?	
Party Favors?	
Items for attendees to bring (ornament exchange, etc.)	
RSVP Deadline	

Additional Information About the Party

Date to Send Invitations	

Party Guest List

Name	Phone/Email	Invitation Sent	RSVP - Yes	RSVP - No	Dietary Restrictions	Total Attending

Christmas Party Food

Event:

Type of Food	Food Item	Serving Dish Needed for Food Item	Will Make	Will Purchase	Ordered	Picked-Up

Party/Entertaining "Need Items"

Make a list of items you need to find or acquire or items that you may need help with at a party/gathering you are hosting. This list will allow you to know what you might need if someone asks, "can I bring anything?" Put this form with your party planning sheets for each party.

Item Needed	Person Bringing

Party Details

Party Theme	
Date of Party	
Time of Party	
Location of Party	

Party Details

Number of People	
Who is the Party for?	
Party Favors?	
Items for attendees to bring (ornament exchange, etc.)	
RSVP Deadline	

Additional Information About the Party

Date to Send Invitations	

Party Guest List

Name	Phone/Email	Invitation Sent	RSVP - Yes	RSVP - No	Dietary Restrictions	Total Attending

Christmas Party Food

Event:

Type of Food	Food Item	Serving Dish Needed for Food Item	Will Make	Will Purchase	Ordered	Picked-Up

Party/Entertaining "Need Items"

Make a list of items you need to find or acquire or items that you may need help with at a party/gathering you are hosting. This list will allow you to know what you might need if someone asks, "can I bring anything?" Put this form with your party planning sheets for each party.

Item Needed	Person Bringing

Christmas Events

Just like activities, events play an essential role in celebrating the Christmas season because they allow us to actively participate in events that bring out the true meaning of Christmas for us. Remember, for our planning purposes, events are things you do or attend away from home.

Think about what events are a must-do each Christmas for you and your family. Do you always go to a family dinner? What about office or club parties? Does your best friend hold a cookie exchange each year? Christmas eve or other church services?

Make a list of all the events you plan to attend during the Christmas season this year, and then for each one, fill out an event planning sheet, so you do not forget the little details for each event.

One final reminder, don't forget to add your events to your December calendar!

Christmas Events List

List all the events you are attending outside of your home.

Event Name & Location	Date/Time of Event

Event Planning Sheet

Use this form to plan out each of the activities you will be doing during the Christmas season.

Name of Event	
Date of Event	
Time of Event	
Place of Event	

Event Details

Type of Event	
Cost of Event	
Hostess gift?	
Items to bring (ornament exchange, dessert, gift, etc.)	
Date to Purchase Tickets	

Additional Information About the Event

Date to RSVP (add to calendar)	

Event Planning Sheet

Use this form to plan out each of the activities you will be doing during the Christmas season.

Name of Event	
Date of Event	
Time of Event	
Place of Event	

Event Details

Type of Event	
Cost of Event	
Hostess gift?	
Items to bring (ornament exchange, dessert, gift, etc.)	
Date to Purchase Tickets	

Additional Information About the Event

Date to RSVP (add to calendar)	

Event Planning Sheet

Use this form to plan out each of the activities you will be doing during the Christmas season.

Name of Event	
Date of Event	
Time of Event	
Place of Event	

Event Details

Type of Event	
Cost of Event	
Hostess gift?	
Items to bring (ornament exchange, dessert, gift, etc.)	
Date to Purchase Tickets	

Additional Information About the Event

Date to RSVP (add to calendar)	

Event Planning Sheet

Use this form to plan out each of the activities you will be doing during the Christmas season.

Name of Event	
Date of Event	
Time of Event	
Place of Event	

Event Details

Type of Event	
Cost of Event	
Hostess gift?	
Items to bring (ornament exchange, dessert, gift, etc.)	
Date to Purchase Tickets	

Additional Information About the Event

Date to RSVP (add to calendar)	

Decorating

Decorating at Christmas can be simple or elaborate – the choice is yours. Be truthful with yourself because, if you do not like decorating the whole house, you either need to delegate the duties or just decorate a small portion of your home.

Use the form Room by Room Decorating to write down each area inside your home that you decorate. Include the style or theme, and if you box your items up by a number or letter system, indicate that on the list also.

Use the form Outside Decorating to write down each area outside your home that you decorate. Include the theme, and if you box your items up by a number or letter system, indicate that on the list also.

Utilize the Master Decorating Shopping List form to list out any new items you need to purchase for the upcoming Christmas season related to decorating.

Room by Room Decorating

For each room that you decorate during the Christmas season, make notes about the style or theme you wish to decorate that room this year.

Area/Room	Style or Theme

Outside Decorating

List the areas outside your house to be decorated along with the style or theme you will use in this area. (For example: porch, front door, yard, mailbox, etc.)

Area to Decorate	Style or Theme

Master Decorating Shopping List

Item	Room	Purchased

Cleaning

Christmas may seem like a long way off, but with some planning, you can accomplish your cleaning goals.

The goal is that by Thanksgiving, you have deep cleaned your house so you can concentrate on just the basics from Thanksgiving through New Year's Day.

The first step is to break your house into five areas. Under each area, list what in each room needs attention to be deep cleaned. List out as many small things as you can so, no one job is too big.

Work on different tasks for 15 minutes at a time using your timer until all the tasks are complete. Your Christmas cleaning and decluttering may take days, weeks, or even months, but that is ok; the goal is to work a little bit as often as you can to have your house ready for the Christmas season.

Room/Area Cleaning List

Make a list of the things that need to be cleaned, decluttered, etc. in the room.

ROOM/AREA:

Task	Completed	Task to be delegated	Task	Completed	Task to be delegated

Room/Area Cleaning List

Make a list of the things that need to be cleaned, decluttered, etc. in the room.

ROOM/AREA:

Task	Completed	Task to be delegated	Task	Completed	Task to be delegated

Room/Area Cleaning List

Make a list of the things that need to be cleaned, decluttered, etc. in the room.

ROOM/AREA:

Task	Completed	Task to be delegated	Task	Completed	Task to be delegated

Room/Area Cleaning List

Make a list of the things that need to be cleaned, decluttered, etc. in the room.

ROOM/AREA:

Task	Completed	Task to be delegated	Task	Completed	Task to be delegated

Room/Area Cleaning List

Make a list of the things that need to be cleaned, decluttered, etc. in the room.

ROOM/AREA:

Task	Completed	Task to be delegated	Task	Completed	Task to be delegated

Traveling

Traveling during the Christmas season can take on different aspects. You could be traveling for an hour or two to your parent's house or across the country. For some, it may mean a vacation during the holiday season. No matter what your ultimate destination is, if it more than 30 minutes from your home, you need to plan your trip.

Use the form Traveling During Christmas to list out all the places you will be traveling to during the season. Include trips of 30 minutes or longer.

Use the form Christmas Travel To-Do List to make a list of all the things you must do for EACH trip. The little details can create havoc if you forget. For instance, forgetting to have the mechanic check out your vehicle before a long road trip or forgetting to reserve the kennel for your pet.

Traveling During Christmas

Make a list of all the places you will be traveling to this Christmas season and how you will be getting there. This will let you plan out other aspects of your holiday plans also.

Date of Travel	Destination	Method of Transportation

Christmas Travel To-Do List

Make a list of "to-do" items for holiday travel. Think of things you wish you would have done on past trips like getting gas before Christmas day, taking more activities for the kids, etc.

	Action Item	Put on Calendar	Called and Reserved	Copied Confirmation and placed in Travel File
1				
2				
3				
4				
5				
6				
7				
8				
9				
10				
11				

Christmas Travel To-Do List

Make a list of "to-do" items for holiday travel. Think of things you wish you would have done on past trips like getting gas before Christmas day, taking more activities for the kids, etc.

	Action Item	Put on Calendar	Called and Reserved	Copied Confirmation and placed in Travel File
1				
2				
3				
4				
5				
6				
7				
8				
9				
10				
11				

Christmas Travel To-Do List

Make a list of "to-do" items for holiday travel. Think of things you wish you would have done on past trips like getting gas before Christmas day, taking more activities for the kids, etc.

	Action Item	Put on Calendar	Called and Reserved	Copied Confirmation and placed in Travel File
1				
2				
3				
4				
5				
6				
7				
8				
9				
10				
11				

SHARE YOUR IDEAS & LEARN NEW IDEAS.

Become part of the

Christmas Organizing Community

Visit Christmas Organizing's website to sign up for our newsletter, read blog posts, connect via social media, listen to the Christmas Joy podcast, join the Candy Cane Club and much more! www.ChristmasOrganizing.com

Plus these online resources

w w w . c h r i s t m a s o r g a n i z i n g . c o m

THANK YOU!

I would like to personally thank you for purchasing the
Christmas Organizing Planner.
Your continued support of Christmas Organizing means more than you will ever
know. If you have any questions, please reach out to me via email at
kblair@christmasorganizing.com or the contact form at
www.christmasorganizing.com

*Merry Christmas from the
Christmas Coach.
Krisann*

Reminders for Christmas 2021

Made in the USA
Columbia, SC
30 September 2020

21778808R00089